THE UNOFFICIAL

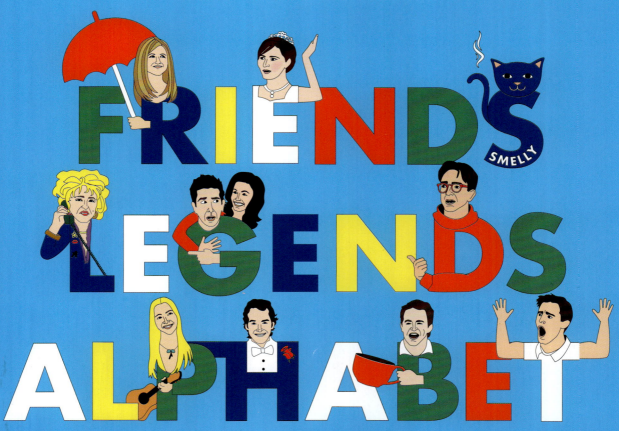

Words by Robin Feiner

Aa

A is for **A**my Greene. Rachel's second-favorite sister and maybe the hottest girl Joey has ever hated. Amy isn't going to win any Aunt of the Year awards after getting Emmett ... Ella ... EMMA's ears pierced while on baby-sitting duty.

Bb

B is for Richard **B**urke. It's easy to see why this charming ophthalmologist with the manly moustache could have been perfect for Monica. Just ignore the 21-year age gap, his desire for no more kids, and his tight friendship with Monica's dad!

Cc

C is for Chandler Bing. Or Ms. Chanandler Bong, according to his TV Guide subscription. Could Chandler BE any more sarcastic? Though known for stepping so far over the line it becomes a dot to him, he's always there for his friends. Legend.

Dd

D is for **D**avid.
The Scientist Guy almost comes up with the solution to win Phoebe's heart. Smooth and suave? Nope! Stammering, smart and sweet? Definitely. Oh, what might have been had he not gone to Minsk with Max for work.

Ee

E is for **E**mily Waltham. Cheerio! This British bride is one of Ross' three wives, ready for a happy life in the United States after their U.K. wedding. But that was before Ross awkwardly said Rachel's name instead of hers during their vows!

Ff

F is for **F**rank Buffay Jr. Phoebe's sweet yet simple half-brother is married to Alice, his former high school teacher. Luckily for them, Phoebe acts as surrogate mother to their triplets – Frank Jr. Jr., Leslie and a surprise daughter whom they name Chandler!

Gg

G is for Ross Geller. We were on a break! Spray tans. Leather pants. And breakup letters that are 18 pages ... front and back! These don't mix well with this nerdy paleontologist. But his love for Rachel is just legendary. He's her lobster!

Hh

H is for Mike **H**annigan. Crap Bag! If only all blind dates ended in this much happiness. His quirkiness and musical ability make him a great husband for Phoebe, and his competitiveness a great table tennis opponent for Monica.

Ii

I is for Isabella Rossellini. Mamma mia! When this legendary beauty finds out she didn't make Ross' final list of celebrity crushes, she passes on his "once in a lifetime opportunity." If only she hadn't just bumped him from her list of goofy coffee house guys.

Jj

J is for **J**anice.
OH. MY. GOD. With her iconic voice, you can hear Chandler's nasal on-again, off-again ex-girlfriend coming a mile away. When she can't take the hint, Chandler buys an expensive ticket to Yemen just to escape her.

Kk

K is for **K**atie (Marcel the Monkey). Marcel, whose real name is Katie, is a white-headed capuchin Ross adopts. But once this monkey develops a humping habit, Ross is forced to say goodbye to his legendary friend.

Ll

L is for Este**l**le **L**eonard. I know, I know, you weren't expecting someone so fantastically beautiful. The head of the Estelle Leonard Talent Agency is proper New Yawk. Pity she's not good at actually landing Joey any acting jobs!

Mm

M is for **M**onica Geller. I know! A neat freak with a competitive streak, Ross' younger sister and Rachel's longtime roommate has a legendary Type A personality. But it's her maternal nature, especially at Thanksgiving, that makes her a favorite among her friends.

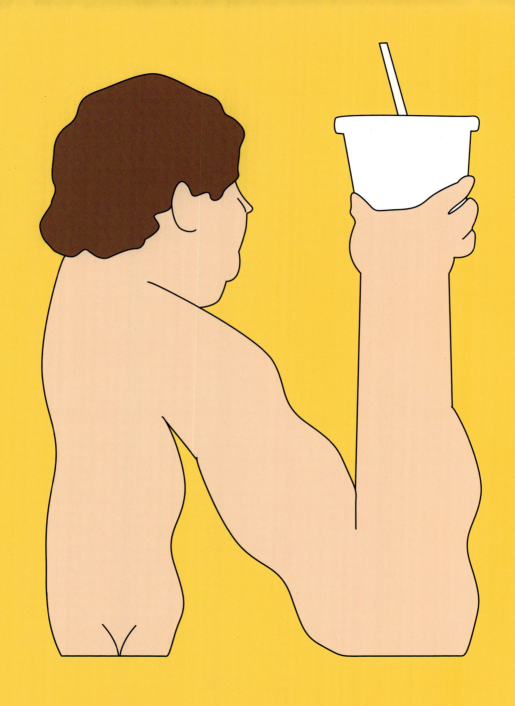

N is for Ugly **N**aked Guy. This neighbor is curiously open, just like his curtains. From laying kitchen tile to using his Thighmaster and gravity boots in the nude, this former Cute Naked Guy gives the gang eyeful after eyeful from his apartment across the street.

Oo

O is for Old Yeller. "Happy family gets a dog, frontier fun!" Right? Oh, Pheebs! Learning that her mom turned off the TV before the end of this movie, she gets a rude shock when she finally watches the ending!

Pp

P is for **P**hoebe Buffay. Or is that Princess Consuela Banana-Hammock? From describing life as "floopy" to fighting with her fire alarm, Phoebe's eccentricity is second to none. Her pearls of wisdom and selflessness make her a truly legendary friend.

Q is for The **Q**uiz. The legendary showdown: Joey and Chandler versus Monica and Rachel, battling it out for the girls' apartment. Michael Flatley, Lord of the Dance. Althea. Big Fat Goalie. Maurice, the Space Cowboy. But what exactly is Chandler's job?

Qq

Rr

R is for **R**achel Greene. The one with 'that' hair. Rachel gets by with some help from her friends before getting one of those "job things" at Central Perk. She finally gets her happy ending with Ross – just don't let her make a trifle!

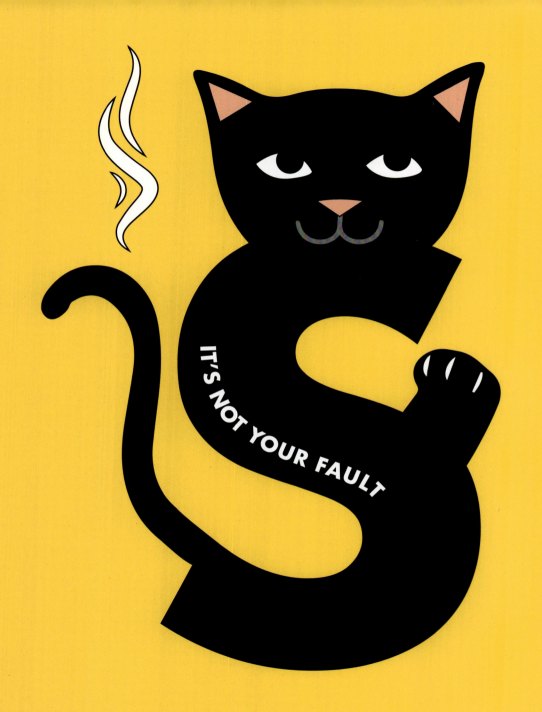

Ss

S is for Smelly Cat.
Go on, sing it loud! "Smelly Cat, Smelly Cat, what are they feeding you? Smelly Cat, Smelly Cat, it's not your fault!" This absolute tune is a staple in Phoebe's Central Perk sets, despite it not being very popular.

T is for Joey **T**ribbiani. How you doin'? Joey's a handsome yet struggling actor who loves women as much as he loves sandwiches, and doesn't share food! This legendary Italian–American puts loyalty to his five friends above all.

Tt

Uu

U is for Gunther.
Ah, Gunther, with his brightly-bleached blond hair and undying love for Rachel. Although seemingly always around, this Dutch-speaking Central Perk manager never fully breaks into the circle of friends. Hey Chandler, what's Gunther's last name?

Vv

V is for Jean-Claude **V**an Damme. The Muscles from Brussels. Wham Bam Van Damme. This legendary action movie superstar kicks his way into the friends' lives for a brief moment, causing Rachel and Monica to compete for his attention.

Ww

W is for **Will** Colbert. Co-founder of the I Hate Rachel Greene Club, Will overcomes his love of complex carbohydrates to go from chunky high schooler to rich and thin. Too bad he never gets invited back for Thanksgiving.

Xx

X is for Janine Lacroi**x**. She's hot. Joey's loveable. What could go wrong? Plenty for these short-term roommates! This Aussie bombshell blessing becomes a curse when she tells Joey to ditch Chandler ("blah") and Monica ("too loud"). Of course, loyal Joey sends her packing.

Yy

Y is for **Y**asmine and Dick. The chick and the duck were like children to juvenile adults Joey and Chandler. Initially a gift from Joey, Chandler names the chick after 'Baywatch' star Yasmine Bleeth before getting his little love stuck in the VCR.

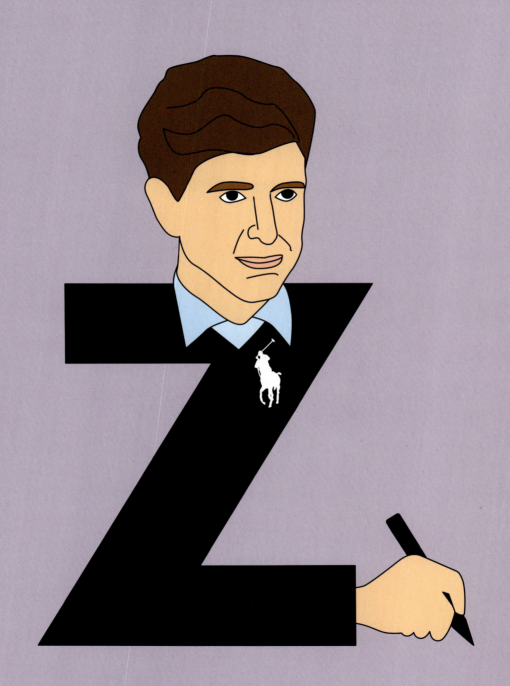

Zz

Z is for **Z**elner. Rachel's straight-laced boss at Ralph Lauren puts up with a lot of her shenanigans. If it weren't for his son's love of dinosaurs and Ross' job as a paleontologist, Rachel could have ended up in Paris.

The ever-expanding legendary library

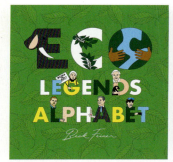

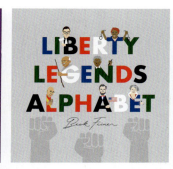

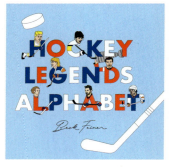

EXPLORE THESE LEGENDARY ALPHABETS & MORE AT WWW.ALPHABETLEGENDS.COM

FRIENDS LEGENDS ALPHABET
www.alphabetlegends.com

Published by Alphabet Legends Pty Ltd in 2020
Created by Beck Feiner
Copyright © Alphabet Legends Pty Ltd 2020

UNICEF AUSTRALIA
A portion of the Net Proceeds from the sale of this book are donated to UNICEF.

9780648962830

The right of Beck Feiner to be identified as the author and illustrator of this work has been asserted by her in accordance with the Copyright Amendment (Moral Rights) Act 2000.

This work is copyright. Apart from any use as permitted under the Copyright Act 1968, no part may be reproduced, copied, scanned, stored in a retrieval system, recorded or transmitted, in any form or by any means, without the prior use of the publisher.

The unofficial Friends Legends Alphabet is a fan publication and tribute to the famous TV series Friends. It has not been officially endorsed by the creators, writers or actors of the show.

Printed and made in China.